Unsto

What Fear, Death, and the Cannabis Black Market

Have to Teach Us About Living

By Ashley Jackson

Dedication:

In honor of believing:

Lighting a candle, putting it in the window

And holding the space for perception to shift.

I know you will.

Preface

One day as a senior in high school, I started feeling lousy. Not just an "oh, maybe I'm catching a cold" kind-of-lousy. No, this was a "something is radically wrong" moment.

My mother worked for a family practice doctor. Our entire family was deeply ingrained in Western medicine, from the time my great-grandfather invented the jaundice box to long past the moment I came stumbling into the doctor's office, desperately seeking my mother's help.

I looked pleadingly into my mother's eyes. I was adamant that something was terribly wrong, but my mother almost laughed it off. I was a seventeen-year-old girl, after all. Everything was about drama, right?

Wrong.

After she sent me to the back room to lay down, I fought my panic and fell asleep. Later, when I awoke to a guttural voice screaming, I was surprised to find that it was me. Panicked, the staff gave me an ultrasound and discovered that my appendix was rupturing.

I yelled "10 plus!" when the doctor asked about my pain on a scale from one to ten, and it took a shot of Demerol to even get to the operating room at the hospital.

I remembered coming out of surgery thinking, *What in the world? Why didn't my mother believe me?*

It really didn't have to do with my mom. Or me.

It had to do with the idea that as a western society, we don't trust the individual to know what is good for them, even when that person knows something is terribly wrong. I saw it as unconscious. It was an outmoded level of thinking that is still entrenched in our families and communities, but especially at the highest levels of schools, the medical care systems, and our government. It's creating wasted lives, broken laws, and desperate answers instead of the alternative we are all seeking.

I got well over the appendix episode, but I hadn't learned to listen to my body or overcome my fear about making the right decisions. Someone else was always the higher authority and knew better than I did. I didn't know that the cultural ideal of acquiescing to western wisdom would come to haunt my every step and bring me to the brink of death.

What I'm about to share with you is how fear, death, and the black market have something to teach us about really living.

Chapter One: Twisting in the Gut

I was raised in the middle of nowhere, Idaho near the Utah border. Now, let me give you a microscope. In this area, there were only three things that thrived: the Mormons, the KKK, and the potato farmers, although not particularly in that order. My father, while not a member of the KKK, was a staunch Republican. He was the proverbial gritty man with the right to bear arms (that you'd definitely have to pry out of his cold, dead fingers).

My community growing up was LDS, commonly called Mormon. Therefore, like the beliefs of every red-blooded Idaho-American Mormon girl in that area, I associated alcohol and any kind of drug (especially a "schedule one drug") with the devil. In our community, this meant hellfire and damnation that would rival a Mississippi Baptist congregation, or at least being judged and ostracized into the shame corner and killing yourself.

I never picked up a cigarette, let alone pot, meth, or any other street drug. I drank alcohol a few times, and was only exposed to Western medicine in ways that I thought had helped me, like aspirin for a headache.

Fast forward five years later to December 2010. I left Texas, where I had been living for about a year, to go to work at the National Finals Rodeo in Las Vegas. I worked in promotions for the events. An associate from the rodeo and I stopped into a McDonald's for a hot coffee and a chat.

Who knew a chat at McDonald's could almost kill you?

It was there in that small but bustling restaurant that I acquired e-coli from bad creamer.

I didn't go to the hospital even though the other person I was with did. Why? Well, he was headed back to Texas when the bug attacked him mid-plane. Apparently, he was rushed from the airport to the hospital, where he remained for nearly three weeks.

That gentleman and I weren't close, so I wasn't aware of his hospitalization until months later when his wife called me. Instead, I struggled with what I thought was surely a bad case of food poisoning. I went through weeks of nasty, severe-stomach-flu symptoms, which never settled down or went away. Intense pain, fierce vomiting, fever, nausea, and cramping became my daily companions. Not the kinds of friends I invite into my space.

Four months later, I moved from Texas to California. I lived in the most abundant food state in the nation but I now feared food. Inside my little California paradise, I couldn't keep anything inside of me. Each time I ate, whether a lot or a little, my body rejected it. Even the first swallow had me running for the bathroom. I began to lose an extreme amount of weight. It was the best diet in the world--if one wanted to look sickly and emaciated. Worse, my brain felt fuzzy, and I needed my brain.

Obviously, being thirty pounds underweight was unattractive, so I worried how this would affect my relationship with my new partner. When I met him I was bubbly, bright, witty, and strong. I was unstoppable. A few days later, however, I became the opposite. My heart and mind were confused. I felt dull, sad, irritable, and weak. The shame of, "who would want someone like this?" crept into my thoughts. Not really knowing how sick I was, I proceeded with the relationship, but it was impossible to hide. After a while, my illness affected every single aspect of my life.

Food is the giver of life. It not only nourishes the cells in our bodies, but also our brains. I was the cowgirl entrepreneur with big ideas. My ideas had been valued and utilized many times over. Many people benefited from them. Lately, however, I could barely drag myself out of bed, much less think with the brilliance I needed to run my rapidly growing business and consult for others.

Calling my mom often for guidance, I also sought out multiple western medicine doctors. That's what I had always been taught, right? The doctors *know*. They have all of this training and technology. They will be able to diagnose you properly and heal you.

The first doctor I visited tried to put me on antidepressants, the second one told me I had leaky gut, and the third one told me I had ulcers. One even said, "Ma'am, this is in your mind. You'll have to control your anxiety or it will never go away."

I rolled my eyes each time, then got into my car with tears streaming down my face. As I left yet another office, I was torn between seeking more doctors asking them about ads I'd heard on the TV that said, "we will help you poop, but while you're pooping you may have seizures or, better yet, you may die."

Oh my God! How is it I am seeking something so illogical?

My fear increased. Why was it I never got better since Vegas? The doctors seemed to ignore that, or thought it was somehow funny, or in my head. They did small workups on me and sent me on my way with a quick diagnosis and always, always some pharmaceutical pill. Still, their diagnoses didn't make sense, and neither did my severe physical and now mental aversion to food. Before the rodeo in Vegas, I never had a problem eating. I wasn't bulimic or anorexic a day in my life. I had immensely enjoyed food. . . and my curves.

As my tangible aversion to eating increased, however, I had to fight harder to get my life back. I battled for as much normalcy as I could muster, yet my behavior was not normal. At friends' get-togethers, I took food and casually threw it away when no one was looking, or fed it to a happy animal under the table. The reaction in my gut was often too severe for even a single bite of food. I knew I couldn't survive without eating, but I was in agony only a minute or two after I swallowed. Anxiety connected to eating grew with each bite. After one such party I came home and sat on my bed and slumped over. I couldn't continue this way.

Maybe it really is in my head?

Chapter Two: The Definition of Insanity

I thought maybe it was time I saw a shrink, so I did. I walked into her office and she looked me up and down. Within moments of me describing what was going, on she declared,

"It sounds like you need an antidepressant. You will be a whole new woman!"

Well, I couldn't wait to be that whole, new woman. Even though I was skeptical during my last encounter with a doctor and a prescription that looked like this, I was in desperation mode. I decided to attempt to embrace her recommend and hope for the best. *Thank you, Jesus!* I thought, and with revived hope, I tore open the package from the pharmacy. I hoped this magic pill blessed by Western medicine would cure me, and I waited for it to kick in. Because I literally had nothing in my body at that point, it didn't take as long for its effects to work.

I felt completely numb for two weeks. I was so emotionally dead, one could almost think I was getting better. There were no panic attacks and no horrific thoughts; I just felt nothing. Yet, when I tried to eat while on the Xanax, I had the same violent gut spasms, except now I just didn't really care.

Shocked, I cried as I finally flushed the pills down the toilet. My pain was exceeding my fear. It was excruciating, and I couldn't live this way anymore.

I desperately started researching on Google, because they said Google knew everything.

That's when I learned about words like "naturopaths" and "holistic practitioners." When I read these words for the first time, my brain had no files to display to explain them. Instead, my curiosity took over and I devoured all the research I found. After reading the first page, I felt in my gut that if I explored these words, they might have an answer.

Did you know holistic medicine is a form of healing that considers the whole person--body, mind, spirit, and emotions--in the quest for optimal health and wellness? I hadn't known that. It was radically different from my experiences with western doctors. I learned about some of the protocols that naturopaths recommended, but I wasn't sure I was willing to try anything on my own.

I sought out a holistic practitioner. In one appointment, she asked me at least a hundred more questions than any western doctor I had previously seen. She inquired about situations and how I felt. She delved deeply, and though her questions didn't always make sense, I could tell they were leading somewhere. She asked how things smelled, or if I remembered anything odd about certain foods. I was blown away.

This doctor was interested in my whole being, which I ultimately found out was what all ancient cultures did to determine absolute health. *Thanks, Google.* Other societies brought a human in and connected at the deepest levels to create emotional, physical, and mental balance for optimal wellness.

As she communicated with me, I knew I was not just a symptom in this woman's office to be covered up by a pill. I was not just a problem to be solved and shooed away. I was a person, and a whole being that needed her help. I remember her eyes glistened with compassion as she listened to my insane stories. I felt her hear me. Something inside of me said, "trust."

I later realized this was the practiced talent of a smart practitioner. Her name was Karen.

Fully clothed, I laid down on a table and she said, "Let me try something."

"Okay," I agreed. By this time I had already felt that if anyone could do something to save my life, this woman could. I had so much empathy for chronically ill humans, and while laid there, I thought of them for some reason. I had an intense desire not to be one of them.

That was when this holistic practitioner began to push on my belly in a spot just below my right ribs. As she did so, she began to ask me questions.

It was like a mute button went on. I saw her lips moving, but that deafening numbness that closed in when my pain was high took over.

My fears, her pushing, or both suddenly seized my mind. "Ouch!" I cried out so quickly and loudly that I startled her. I was thrown horrifically into the nauseous state I'd been fighting and succumbing to for so long. Imagine the worst flu multiplied by a hundred, and that was what I generally experienced every time I decided to eat over the last several months.

Now it's happening while some random, holistic medicine woman is pushing on me? Confusion set in, which didn't help me think this phenomenon through.

The brain fog persisted as she continued to massage the same spot. My eyes bulged and tiny sweat beads glistened on my forehead. When Karen pushed harder, I yelped like a stepped-on dog.

My practitioner then looked me straight in the eye and said, "In order to stay alive, you'll need to include marijuana in your daily routine immediately. I also believe this disease, which I would speculate is some form of e-coli, has affected your gallbladder and you'll need it removed."

I stared blankly at her for what felt like five minutes.

What the fuck?

Aloud I managed to stammer, "Without an x-ray? And won't I go to jail?" These two questions came up at the same time. I had never even smoked a cigarette, let alone that "m" word!

Former Mormon girl, remember? My mom worked for a family practice doctor, remember? A whole scene played out in my head. I imagined telling my mother, "hey, I'm going to smoke pot to get better."

That would go over well! I could also just imagine her telling the doctor, "please remove my daughter's gallbladder. . . on request from a holistic practitioner." That's when I saw that doctor saying, "No way, crazy lady, I will do no such thing. And for that matter, marijuana is a gateway drug that may lead to her addiction to opioids or worse!"

My mind raced as tears welled up in my eyes. My body temperature continued increasing to sustain a steady sweat. My shirt was now soaking wet. Smoke filled my mind, but not my lungs.

My greatest fear was coming true. *I have to do drugs!* Marijuana was the kind that the D.A.R.E program told me from the time I was six was as bad as opioids or heroin. Scruff McGruff, the TV commercial crime dog, would surely put me in prison. I had also witnessed too many young people on the streets, addicted to opioids in Idaho, in Texas, and now in California.

I can't be next.

I shuddered at the thought of ingesting or smoking this medicine-drug marijuana, and was quickly reminded of the frail state my body was in. Any movement was painful. I knew the truth: I was slowly dying. I was now forty pounds lighter than my optimal weight.

My entire body was suffering. My cells were crying out for some kind of relief.

Dr. Karen saw my fear, as it was clearly written all across my face; the battle lines were drawn and sections of me were already quartered. She looked me in the eyes and comforted me, assuring me that I would be amazed at the results.

She also gently explained that I could find a dispensary near her office. After her recommendation, however, I didn't hear her any more. I don't even remember leaving her office.

I went home instead of to the dispensary. I sat at the computer, the recommendation for marijuana in my head. Numbly, I looked up holistic practitioners and the prescription of marijuana for extreme nausea. I learned that marijuana had only been deemed illegal in 1918, and that the government of the United States had been producing 60,000 pounds at the time for resale use.

In 1985, the government approved a synthetic form of marijuana called Marinol. In 1990, a man named Miles Herkenham discovered that in every human brain there was a receptor for a thing called cannabinoids. Marijuana produced THC, a tetrahydrocannabinol. It sounded pretty technical, but somehow important.

But why was I learning about all this? And what was I even thinking, putting marijuana in my search engine?

Good God! The Feds could come.

Nevertheless, I saw the pieces now. I was a human, I had a brain, and I was dying. Maybe this could help me. Maybe this wasn't about a leaky gut or uncontrollable anxiety. Maybe my brain and my body had somehow led me to a new, real answer. And maybe my practitioner knew what she was talking about, and I had to start taking this immediately or I would die.

Little did I know the new California partner I was in love with was well-versed in cannabis. He had hidden it well from me because of my fear of drugs and his desire not to lose me. But when he saw my new pot prescription, he obliged to help out. It turned out he was also legally growing in California.

Two hours after my appointment, I was still in my sweaty shirt, in shock. I sat staring at a glass jar filled with plants that looked like coned broccoli. I couldn't believe it. *This is it? You have to be kidding me.* I expected it to be on fire, smell like bleach, or something different than green flowers. I thought it would be so vile that I would gag. It turned out that it actually smelled good.

Plant medicine. *Can it be true?*

I found no relief from staring at the jar, so I asked kindly if my partner could help me take the leap. My heart pounded. There was more perspiration. Was I really going to do this?

He rolled me a joint.

I closed my eyes.

He lit the joint.

And I inhaled.

The first time, nothing happened. I literally sat there, astonished that I was now on the dark side. I had not been struck by lightning. And sadly, not a single thing was happening in my body. My heart fell.

I went through all of that, and no response? *Great. I'm going to hell, and it didn't even help.*

Chapter Three: The Seeds of Ancient, Working Medicine

I was still alive. When I say nothing happened as I sat in our California apartment, I meant I inhaled, exhaled, and expected my skin to start peeling off. But, no. Nothing.

With my partner's urging, I inhaled again, and what I experienced was nothing short of a miracle. I felt the most incredible relief; a warm, soothing, smooth feeling traveled up my legs and to my head. My brain was confused at first. It tried to tell me, "No! This isn't safe!", but at this point my body and my intuition were so in sync that nothing could stop me, not even my fear. It was like I felt a tiny person sitting in my brain saying, "Just keep breathing. You know how to feel well again."

I sat astonished.

Within twenty minutes of relaxing for the first time in months, I could smell the food that was cooking, which seemed new. Previously I avoided food and its smells, but then I suddenly decided I was brave enough to eat something.

Ah, my first case of the munchies!

The last few months I ate next-to-nothing, and now I ate and drank water. The most glorious miracle was I was able to keep it down.

Wow! My body and my brain were loving it. Extreme relief kicked in. Then the guilt kicked in. I now had a medicine that helped me curb my extreme nausea, but I still thought I was going to hell. . . and possibly jail.

I had, however, overcome my fear and shame. No doubt I could work through my guilt to see that I had followed my intuition. As I continued eating over the next few days, it saved my life.

At age twenty-four, I was shoved into the burdensome opportunity of being a diplomat for cannabis. For the first time, I saw both sides of the issue clearly. Something that I had been told was bad for me and was judged an illegal, immoral substance had revived my senses and had given me my bubbly imagination back.

I went back to the doctor my mom worked for. I was strong enough to drive home and entered his office. As I did so, I trembled inwardly because he was still the all-knowing authority figure of my childhood. Yet I took a breath and I stood my ground, telling him the truth.

He responded as I knew he would, and I saw the disgust cross his face. He hated knowing I was using cannabis, but he also realized that I was finally able to eat. The doctor told me that I needed a dye test that would show if my gallbladder was working or not, but it couldn't happen for a couple of days. In his mind, the crisis had passed and I was no longer in an emergency state. Whether he liked it or not, thanks to the cannabis, I was eating now.

But I knew I needed this test and procedure *yesterday*. So, I begged. Intuitively I knew that somehow this test and the surgery were how my body could heal. This couldn't get started in a few more days. It just couldn't. I looked at him with tears in my eyes and begged him again.

The doctor finally relented. He ordered a test at a medical facility for 4:00pm that afternoon. An hour later, my mom was shocked when the hospital called to schedule an emergency surgery for 6:00am the very next day. Not only was I septic from the e-coli, but they also deemed my gallbladder functioning at only 9%. I was in mortal danger.

When I went in to have my diseased gallbladder removed, my body had a total meltdown going under anesthesia because of the declined state of health it was in. On the operating table, I flatlined, sending everyone into a panic.

In this case, I was very fortunate that Western medicine was available. Thanks to the surgical team's life-saving measure, I'm here now, but it was only because a holistic doctor showed me my ability to begin my healing process with cannabis. I know to this day I could not have survived had I not finally had some nutrients in my system for a few days before the surgery.

That experience of life and near-death was so profound that I knew without a shadow of a doubt that Karen and cannabis saved my life. Without them, I wouldn't have been able to eat to begin healing, nor maintain the sanity I needed to heal my disease. I learned how extreme disease could make my brain foggy and my pain nearly unbearable. And I learned life was worth risking my old beliefs for.

My vibrant health returned, and I continue to use cannabis as needed. I felt grateful and lucky I was able to recognize my fear and move through it to the other side.

My whole situation shifted my world view when I was twenty-four. Today I am thirty-one. I sell cowboy boots for a living, consult with businesses on marketing and strategy, and travel across the country. I have a blast being alive, and I am extremely passionate about what I do. I also love speaking on following your intuition.

Imagine that.

In my Colorado travels for my boot business a couple years ago, I was privileged to be the manager at a western store that was being revamped. I hired a young lady named Tiffany. This beautiful woman was very shy at first, but she shared with me from day one that she had been in the military and was recently honorably discharged with great accolades and hopes. She also shared that she was struggling to realign with life. She felt like she had PTSD.

"I'm afraid often," she admitted. "I experience sheer terror at times, like when I hear fireworks. All night long, I will stay up and lock myself in the closet with a gun, feeling I may need to use it."

"What are you doing for this anxiety?" I asked. I needed to know I was hiring someone I could count on, and that she was taking steps to manage her condition.

Deep within me, I also felt compassion. I'd had a kind of anxiety regarding an "outer enemy", too. Hers was bad guys, and mine had been food, and though they seemed far from one another, the symptoms and the realities were radically the same.

I felt like we all had PTSD, a trigger of sorts from a past trauma just from being human and in relationships with other humans and nature. It typically was not what was happening in the moment, but how one dealt with their triggers that mattered. Most of all, I knew the feeling of being terrorized and not having a solution.

Tiffany disclosed that she was seeing a therapist that had prescribed her Xanax at one point and Adderall at another. She didn't like how she felt on either substance, so she wasn't taking any of them now. She actually feared all of it. I related to that as well from my past experience, and so I was surprised when Tiffany also admitted she felt extremely depressed. She was grateful for the job, but wanted me to know she could only work a few hours every day.

I hired her anyway, and observed her for the next five months. I saw her puffy eyes when she came into work after crying. I saw her often despondent, and desperate for help.

In the meantime, I was panicking inside. My fear was back. You see, fear doesn't ever go completely away from any human's life; it just gets dealt with, whether rationally or irrationally. This one was beginning to feel a little irrational. I couldn't sit on my knowledge and not help her. She was suffering like I had been, just in a different way.

What do I do with this beautiful young woman? Do I help her? Do I share my story with her? Will I go to jail? Am I a good person either way? Will she even care about my story? Will I feel stupid and realize it's not that great a story to tell?

As I was having this continued inner battle with myself one morning at the store, Tiffany walked in. I could tell she'd had one of those nights, locked in her closet with her gun as her companion and nemesis.

The doctor that I was not *and* the doctor that I was took a bold step into the fear.

I took a breath and invited Tiffany to step outside with me for a few minutes. I shared with her what I had been able to accomplish by facing my greatest fear. I told her of my situation precisely, and my personal challenge to make the decision to try cannabis for fear of being wrong. I shared how I had created health with cannabis as a key partner. I had gone back to being unstoppable. I then shared how I had needed to do lots of research to find facts, and that maybe if she was open to it, if she asked her therapist for a recommendation, she could do the same.

"Actually," Tiffany admitted, "I did ask my therapist. She can't prescribe that for me, as the government doesn't smile on that. I'm a Vet; the Feds pay for us. Feds hate Mary Jane."

More panic rose in me, and straight fear looked me in the eye.

I decided to continue taking a risk and became soft, authentic, and vulnerable; these were all things I had picked up over an entire decade of gleaning from the legendary Brené Brown, Oprah, and more recently Jen Sincero and Rachel Hollis. In two minutes, I found myself offering her the opportunity for education at the local dispensary, accompanied by me.

Tiffany politely declined, but I knew I had planted a seed.

Your body, your temple, and your vessel are unique. When you feel out of whack, out of sorts, or diseased, ask yourself, "Is there something I don't know that could assist me? Could what I know and how I feel not be in alignment? Are there beliefs in me that are making it hard to live the fullest expression of myself?"

Then listen.

I promise, your body has all your answers. The key is to find other humans who can keep you in the question long enough to find your answers and then support you to act on them. It doesn't have to be cannabis; it's not the answer for everyone. But it is the answer for many, and it's important to have the courage to find out.

I moved back to Utah, and about a month after I planted that seed, Tiffany started to message me from Colorado. She was coy at first, but finally came out and said she was ready to go to the marijuana dispensary. My heart expanded. Tears welled up in my eyes as I read her message. I really just wanted her to feel well again. I had seen so much of her pain from trauma.

"Girl," I texted, "way to face your fear!!"

She went to the dispensary, and while they didn't offer "medical advice" they were able to share with her options that were working for other PTSD patients. They also asked her questions, just like my holistic doctor in California had asked me. Tiffany started taking the medicine, and within two days she was at the gym for the first time in half a year. Slowly and steadily, her words became more positive and each message she sent me was more grounded.

The last one I got was this:

"Ashley, thank you so much for helping me when no one else could. My terrorizing PTSD episodes have become controllable and I can clearly see a path to heal. I couldn't have done this without you."

Notice she used a word here that I believe really defines the human experience: control. It can be contorted into a bad thing by society, but essentially control is what determines how we feel. If Tiffany could better control her PTSD triggers and episodes, she could feel better.

Could this also be an answer for many others who are struggling? Was it necessary for cannabis to be legal in some states and illegal in others? These profound questions, and many others, hung heavy in my mind.

Chapter Four : Personal Research

I really wanted to know the answers to these questions, so I decided to conduct interviews and do more Google research.

The Encyclopedia Britannica had this to say about my search for marijuana:

"Marijuana has long been considered valuable as an analgesic, an anesthetic, an antidepressant, an antibiotic, and a sedative. Although it was usually used externally (e.g., as a balm, etc), in the 19th century ce its tips were sometimes administered internally to treat gonorrhea and angina pectoris. Marijuana's effects vary, depending upon the strength and amount consumed, the setting in which it is taken, and the experience of the user" (https://www.britannica.com/science/marijuana).

This resource also told me that there have been references to this plant as early as 2700 BCE, and to me that was a long time ago. My perplexed brain had to pause right there. How could America, this country of freedom that I lived in that was barely 200 years old have a stranglehold on the use of this plant? Why was it so suppressed in our society?

I went on to learn more about the man I referenced earlier, Miles Herkenham. He wasn't the first person to study cannabis scientifically. For decades questions had been raised, especially since the mid-1960s, when THC was first isolated and produced synthetically. Research was directed toward identifying the short-term and long-term physical effects of marijuana.

In the late 20th and early 21st centuries, medical research revealed various therapeutic effects of marijuana and THC. They were found to be useful in lowering internal eye pressure in persons suffering from glaucoma and in alleviating nausea and vomiting caused by chemotherapeutic drugs used to treat cancer patients and those with AIDS. Marijuana also had been found to reduce the muscle pain associated with multiple sclerosis and to prevent epileptic seizures in some patients (https://www.britannica.com/science/marijuana). If Britannica was telling me this, it was common knowledge. Why couldn't the medical industry see this information and make wise decisions?

My research led me to the knowledge that international trade in marijuana and hashish was first placed under controls during the International Opium Convention of 1925. By the late 1960s, most countries had enforced restrictions on trafficking and using marijuana and hashish, and had imposed severe penalties for their illegal possession, sale, or supply.

Beginning in the 1970s, some countries and jurisdictions reduced the penalty for the possession of small quantities. The Netherlands was a notable example; the government decided to tolerate the sale of small amounts of marijuana (https://www.britannica.com/place/Netherlands). Other European countries also began debating the decriminalization of so-called "soft drugs", including marijuana.

I was surprised to learn that in the United States, several states passed legislation in the late 1970s and early '80s to fund research on or to legalize the medicinal use of marijuana, though some of these statutes were later repealed or lapsed (https://www.britannica.com/science/medical-cannabis). Renewed decriminalization efforts in the 1990s led to the legalization of medicinal marijuana in more than a dozen states, including Alaska, Arizona, California, Colorado, Nevada, Oregon, and Washington.

In 2001, however, the U.S. Supreme Court ruled against the use of marijuana for medical purposes. Later that year, Canada passed legislation easing restrictions on medicinal marijuana. That country's new regulations included licensing marijuana growers to produce the drug for individuals with terminal illnesses or chronic diseases.

In 2009, U.S. Attorney General Eric Holder issued a new set of guidelines for federal prosecutors in states where the medical use of marijuana was legalized. The policy shift mandated that federal resources were to be focused primarily on prosecuting illegal use and trafficking of marijuana, thereby rendering cases of medical use in which those individuals in possession of the drug were clearly in compliance with state laws, less prone to excessive legal investigation.

It seems that humans have been using cannabis intuitively and ingeniously for far longer than the USA and its politics have been around. The broader sweep of history helps us realize that now is the time to wake up to the idea that cannabis has healing properties that can be used for good.

Plant medicine in general seems to be undervalued. I won't go in the "big pharma' controversy yet. Since going on my own cannabis journey, I have explored other areas of plant medicine and found that, like anything, when properly used and administered, these substances have extremely positive effects.

Chapter Five: The Irony

Since my life was saved through the miracle of cannabis, I found my voice, my courage, and myself again. This gutsy girl in cowboy boots has now had the opportunity to travel through much of the country. I've met incredible people from all walks of life. What has surprised me is the vast number of people who are affected by chronic anxiety, or chronic pain and illness.

Because I'm no longer afraid to talk about it, many of these people have shared how cannabis has eased their symptoms. And here's the clincher: to the same degree as I've personally experienced, and for some even greater, it has eased symptoms to the point of making their lives *livable* again.

Livable, that is, until the cops come.

As Shakespeare said, "there's the rub." There is great irony in the fact that I've met hundreds of extremely responsible, law-abiding citizens who are forced to do something illegal in order to live as normal lives as possible.

I can't help but compare this to Prohibition in the United States from 1920 to 1933. Normally "responsible" citizens, whose families and cultures had grown up around alcohol in worship rituals, holiday traditions, or a bit of daily imbibing were forced to choose to go without or purchase illegally from a growing black market.

Prohibition forced many unexpected consequences. Hypocrisy was widespread. Government officials often imbibed in bootlegged alcohol, even as they were passing laws to continue the "noble experiment." People trusted their leaders less. In addition, according to PBS, the economic expectation of the nation was that Prohibition would somehow create greater economic fortune in entertainment, real estate, and the development of jobs and neighborhoods. Instead, the country experienced a marked decline in these industries. State budgets also suffered from the loss of tax excises once levied against alcohol and its imbibers. In fact, New York state lost 75% of its revenues once derived from liquor taxes (https://newyorkbeerproject.wordpress.com/2015/07/16/sunday-brew-edition-10/). It crippled the state's budget.

There were two other major consequences I feel need to be discussed, as I've watched them unfold in our country in regard to cannabis. It is widely believed that Prohibition actually led to the rise of alcoholism and the use of alternative substances. Even worse, since items on the black market were not subject to quality control, substitute and alternative alcohols poisoned thousands to their deaths.

The black market created an epic rise in organized crime. Well-accounted histories detail the growth of mobsters and bootleggers, often in collusion with government officials to keep their highways open for the demand of the average citizen.

A Journey Of Everyday Unstoppable Warriors

There was a reason Prohibition was repealed. Everyday citizens should not have to become criminals to get what they need.

I myself began using cannabis illegally until it became legal in California. As I traveled to other states for business, however, I suddenly descended to the irresponsible status of "criminal" if I was caught. Still, I held my own personal judgments about widespread legalization until I heard about a man named Dave Cromar. My close friend Sydnee introduced me to him and his story. Meeting Dave made me immediately rethink all of my judgments.

Dave was the father of several young children in Utah. In 2009, one child began suffering with multiple seizures the day after he received his vaccinations. Vaccinations were required to attend Utah public schools unless exempt under medical, religious, or philosophical reasons. In other words, for parents these routine shots were a given. One day Holden was a normal, healthy two-year-old boy, and the next his life had completely changed for the worse.

Imagine being a parent, holding your child who is seizing uncontrollably. Then imagine having to endure your child's suffering between forty and a hundred times a day. Dave told me it was excruciating, and emotions filled his voice as he spoke. It literally affected every aspect of his family's lives; work, school, meals, and so much more. The hardest part was all of them had to watch Holden suffer.

In 2013, they consulted a neurosurgeon.

Dave told me how the Western medical doctors wanted to remove a piece of his son's brain to stop the seizures. The dangers of such a brain surgery were very real. Dave and his wife didn't want Holden to risk losing any part of his personality, let alone his life.

"There *had* to be other options," Dave said. So he kept researching and saw a story of a girl named Charlotte in Colorado, and how cannabis was helping her with seizures.

Although a bit shocking to Dave, he was looking for last resorts and decided he wanted to try cannabis as a way to stop the seizures before they cut open Holden's brain. The problem was all forms of cannabis were illegal in Utah. At the time, it wasn't even an option for thoroughly vetted medical patients. The Agricultural Hemp Act was still under debate.

Dave could not afford to wait around. Holden's symptoms were present in his face hundreds of times a day. But as a law-abiding citizen, Dave wasn't about to do something illegal that would risk his family. He immediately moved his family to Colorado and put Holden's name on the list to get CBD. They discovered it could be a long time until he was approved. They also discovered that several other families had moved to Colorado at the same time, looking for help for their children. Dave and his wife couldn't wait and watch Holden suffer. They needed to make another move, so they started Holden on THCA. He obtained it from someone in Colorado out of desperation illegally.

Immediately they saw a reduction in Holden's seizures; in fact, it cut the small boy's 40-100 daily seizures in half. With the THCA, Holden had shorter seizures.

"The other great thing," says Dave, "is immediately we saw in increase in his learning and retention. When he was between three and four years old, he learned his colors and letters. He had lost that all by the time he was six. With the THCA, he was able to remember the letters and numbers, and regain access to his cognitive functions." I noticed that Dave's voice was full of emotion again, but this time I heard joy. The THC in the cannabis was giving him his son back, naturally.

"The only thing a Western doctor will look at is 'will this substance reduce seizures?', but as a parent," says Dave, "we see not only seizure reduction, but also cognitive improvement, and a drastic improvement in quality of life and our son's personality. All of these things aren't necessarily measurable to doctors and politicians."

Eventually Dave was able to get access to CBD as well, and added that to Holden's regimen. Things only improved from there.

The most meaningful insight from Dave was this: "One of the greatest gifts of learning about the power of medical cannabis is that really it's just a piece of nutrition that is missing in our lives. It made us take a broader look at our entire lifestyle and ask the questions, 'What are we exposing ourselves to that could be making things worse? And what are we missing that could make things better?"

As Dave's story unfolded, I couldn't imagine this responsible, job-holding dad having to battle with uprooting his family in the midst of his child's serious seizures—all because cannabis couldn't legally be used.

Dave's story, in conjunction with my journey, were what propelled me to write this book. I had first heard about Dave and his son from my friend, and then I followed the story closely on the news. But when I interviewed Dave to get the whole story, the moment I heard his voice my heart pounded. I could feel his sense of anxiety and desperation as he told his story of watching his son be at the mercy of the law.

I could feel that everything changed when he had to deal with a child who was defenseless against seizures. The overwhelming sense of duty and grace Dave exuded was captivating to me. His courage to do the right for thing for someone he loved so fiercely was undoubtedly the strongest I had ever encountered.

Until recently, Dave and his family were active members of the LDS church in Utah, the epicenter of the Mormon faith. Suddenly Dave found himself not only caught between his son's health and the law, but also his faith. The LDS church held a strong stance that medical marijuana should not be legalized in Utah or any other state. Dave and his family fought for legalization so they could bring Holden home again, but it was obvious that it would be years before that could happen.

"It's very confusing for people because they see the benefit, but they also see the Church step in and say, 'Whoa whoa whoa, not in our backyard!" Dave told Fox13, an affiliate based in Salt Lake City on Tuesday, Nov 7, 2018. As Dave shared his story and showed sweet Holden with signs encouraging a change in Utah legislation, people began to talk. A wave of sympathy and compassion washed over the state.

By about 9:00pm that evening, I saw that The Church of Jesus Christ of Latter-day Saints issued a news release. It emphasized its support for relieving human suffering and its concern for the welfare of children.

I would call this a victory. In my opinion, the Mormon Church has definitely been a player in keeping the substance on the 'bad side of the law." With compassion and empathy, I believe it is only a matter of time before one of the church authority's children or grandchildren will need cannabis medicine. It will be interesting to see what happens.

Chapter Six: How Will The Journey Continue?

Because I am publishing this book right in the middle of the "Cannabis Revolution", I am aware that by the next election cycle, things could look drastically different. I hope for Dave and his family, and others like them, that it only continues progressing. The good news for Dave is that I don't think Colorado will go backward on its legality.

Dave is a hero in my book. He had to fight against his religion, the law of his land, his fear, and his moral compass to save his child. His story is gut-wrenching and unfortunately it's not unique. There are too many people who wake up to genuine pain every day. They could be soothed by this plant, but they struggle not knowing if they will ever get it legally.

Fox 13 and KSL, both stations out of Utah, have done small documentaries on Dave and Holden's story, which have been helpful in changing many minds and hearts, like mine.

"Dave," I asked, "if you could go back in time, what would you do differently?"

"I would have looked at this as a first-line treatment, not just a last resort," he said decisively. "Not just a narrow view of THC versus CBD or together, but that there's a whole spectrum of the complete plant. Every strain will react differently with every condition. There is no one answer for everybody. *But*, what comes with medical cannabis is a community of caring people who are willing to understand what you are going through. They say, 'oh, your child is experiencing these symptoms? Oh, here's what we've tried.'"

Because of their willingness to share, Dave said he has been able to use topicals, capsules, vape, and other various delivery methods for more effective results for his son.

Dave also shared another aspect of Holden's journey. "HIPPA makes records shameful. It is hard for patients to access information about their own bodies. "I want to help everyone have access to this safe, benign, and effective plant."

I agreed wholeheartedly, because of what I had learned from so many people over the last few years. Their stories impacted me greatly, to the extent that they always gave me warm chills.

I met a woman named Lacey S., who found out she had breast cancer at twenty-eight. She used cannabis to relieve her nausea from the chemo. She ended up with a double mastectomy and used cannabis lotion on her scars every day. With tears in her eyes, she told me it made the pain manageable; she did not need narcotics.

I met Mary in Wisconsin. Her mother was in late-stage Alzheimer's, and she had been trying desperately to ease her confusion and sadness. Mary found THC patches in Colorado and had to get them shipped illegally to Wisconsin. Mary recounted with me the first time she put one on her mom.

"Within minutes, Mom's eyes became very clear and she called me by name about an hour later. She talked about a dog that had been gone for years and said that perhaps the next day she could go and get a new dog. It's like her will to live was reignited." I was astounded. This was an aspect of the plant I hadn't realized was possible.

Then I met Michelle S., who had been suffering from Crohn's Disease for eight years. Michelle was bedridden and could only walk with a cane. Diagnosed as terminally ill, Michelle decided to explore alternative remedies in a last bid to save her life. One day in her research, Michelle saw an informational video made by a man who claimed to have cured himself with cannabis oil. Intuitively, she says, she knew that was her answer. She is now considered cured and has a normal life.

I sat down with Stormy Simon, former CEO of Overstock.com. She lead a team that came up with the giant red "O". She parted with the company and has gone headlong into the cannabis industry promoting women, marijuana, health, and a combination of all three.

The two of us had a refreshing conversation, during which Stormy explained that due to some of her own health concerns she had to seek out alternative medicine. This lead her on a journey similar to mine. She found out that her body had more answers than she had given it credit for. She felt, listened, and observed her way into feeling better.

Stormy's achievements are nothing short of one of the greatest female CEOs in history. She's gritty. She held every position at Overstock, from warehouse sweat labor to advertising to CEO, all while bravely raising boys as a single mom. I also admire her because before and after she left the company, people said negative things about her, this did not thwart her rise or her leaving. She and Oprah both agree that those who say "who does she think she is?" are probably scared of her power.

The reality is, it is just perception; you choose how you feel about any subject. Mindset is not something taught in life, school, or college. Mindset is something we develop from those we surround ourselves with.

Cannabis now seems to make sense in people's minds, or they immediately desire more information and become creative about the way they handle situations. These open conversations and searches for facts about medicines like cannabis raise things to a level where humans are able to choose based on their needs, not their beliefs.

These are just a few of the personal stories of healing that I've encountered, and I know there are hundreds of thousands, if not millions, more. All of these occurred outside of legal states. How do they get this medicine if it is illegal in most regions? There are other aspects to this story that must be discussed, and not from a moral, religious, or political point of view. This has everything to do with financial ramifications, and we need to address that in regards to law-abiding citizens.

I've now met thousands of people who have a job in the cannabis industry. There are hundreds of sectors of growth that never existed before. I read an article that stated that by 2025 there will be over 642,000 jobs in a $25 billion dollar market (https://news.cannamaps.com/cannabis-initiatives-pass-in-three-of-four-states-in-mid-term-election-cycle/). Just let that sink in.

The ways that Colorado in particular has smartly and effectively handled this "Schedule 1" drug proves to me the huge, double-standard across America.

It's shown me that cannabis needs to be rescheduled.

I'd like to address the elephant in the room, and, no, it's not smoking a joint. Big Pharma wants to keep people in fear so they don't lose money on their manufactured drugs. I don't think this is necessarily a conspiracy theory, but there is a lot of truth in the resistance that is happening in the already multi-billion-dollar industry of manufactured pharmaceutical chemicals.

I don't have to be the one to tell you truths. I'd actually like you to find them for yourself.

In the meantime, as a country full of smart, capable business people and leaders, we need to tackle this issue from economic and long-term benefits-to-losses ratios. My first encounter with marijuana was with someone who produced it legally, but there was an extreme demand across the U.S. for it to be sold illegally.

This black market seems to be a strange problem as we transition through the legality of the plant. Legal states are overflowing with cannabis medicine and money. Neighboring states (like Kansas across from Colorado) are spending millions arresting people at the state line, spending taxpayer money, and perhaps most importantly, fighting a battle that is already lost.

Right now, 29 out of 50 states are legally dispensing medical marijuana. Former President Obama even endorsed marijuana. Mark my words, President Trump is a business man and he will see that cannabis will become a commodity. Resistance is not only futile but is also costly, and Prohibition should have taught us valuable lessons of what happens when a product that should be monitored within an individual is put into the hands of those unafraid to break the law. Instead, I feel that it should be monitored and put into the hands of states to administer and reap the benefits.

I would like to help tell the cannabis story and bring awareness to the wide-spread Cannabis Prohibition that is still going. I am here to be a part of the change to make this medicine more readily available for those who need it.

With Josh McCrimmon, a partner, we created a petition called www.Debate28.org. It calls for the federal government to put an end to the scheduling of this plant in all its forms. I encourage everyone to sign this and be a part of history as we reform our nation. This opportunity is unique and will have a lasting imprint on the future.

I also created a place to share and read stories about cannabis. www.YourCannabisStory.com is an online network sharing real stories of tribulation and triumph directly related to cannabis.

It brings me joy and further inspiration to see people from all over the world post their stories on both websites. There are painful stories as well as so many extremely positive ones. This movement is brilliant because we have to have the courage and foresight to address all the issues that come up.

We can't smother them, but we can't paint over them with a glossy paintbrush, either. There are too many factors, too much money, and too many personal stories of health and healing on the line. It's time for an open discussion.

I have a powerful story to tell about the future of cannabis. I want my voice to raise this question for you: why should cannabis be legal? How can increasing my knowledge about this plant impact my daily life?

At the end of the day, there is only you.

What will you do with the knowledge of medical marijuana and its benefits? I encourage you to be unstoppable by being and staying e informed about cannabis on your own terms. It's very empowering, no matter what your opinion ends up being.

I invite you to become educated about cannabis and all its names, i.e. marijuana, pot, trees, herb, taking a toke, passing a joint, hitting a bong, and more. Know what your children are saying, because I guarantee they've been talking about it, and they might know a lot more than you. Do the research. Talk to people. Have honest conversations. And most of all:

FACE YOUR FEAR.

Be willing to learn.

Be open to change.

Get comfortable with being uncomfortable.

Look at your fear and engage it.

Step into it.

That's the magic of being unstoppable.

Wise humans have said, "For what we fear the most will surely destroy us."

Do you wonder what they mean?

From my own personal experience I can say if you can learn to manage your fear from an informed place, you will see rapid transformation in your life. I wholeheartedly believe that each person has their own answers inside them.

Especially you.

If you have a medical issue, please use your love or your fear of it to propel you into knowledge like Tiffany did. If not for yourself, maybe you'll research it for the sake of the child seizing uncontrollably on the floor while his parent tries to figure out how to move to a different state so he can get the medicine he needs.

Maybe you'll do it for the mother and father who are frantically searching for an answer to their child's cancer. Or maybe you'll do it for the husband who didn't allow his wife to have cannabis, and watched her die of cancer despite chemotherapy, never knowing what may have been. Or perhaps you'll do it for all those beautiful hands knotted and suffering with arthritis.

Mostly I hope you do it for the generations to come. Educate yourself for them, for your children, and your children's children. They will rejoice that their ancestors were brave enough to look fear in the face and inform themselves anyway. Even if it's only a small part of one of your days, try learning about CBD, THC, and THCa. Just use Google. You can do it! Put down the book and try it now!

We all know your fingertips are seconds away from unlimited data. The feds will not come. Humans crave consistent, positive reinforcement that learning and growing are safe. You can aim to hear from those who have had their lives affected by this plant. If you have enough courage, you'll find the good and the bad. Such is life.

I ask that you be open. If you make up your mind in advance that this is bad, sick, and wrong, all of the evidence will have that slant to it. If you choose to have an open mind, you may be amazed at what could show up on your screen.

There is one last thing...

Up until now, no one has portrayed cannabis in a light that is educational; most debates only focus on who is right and who is wrong.

This plant deserves to rise above the pettiness of men and women and be exposed for the gentle healer it can be. Until the federal government is willing to take a stand, misinformation and fake news about cannabis will always be present.

I call for a radical change. It takes courage, intellect, and willpower to overcome fear and become educated about anything, but especially so with cannabis, and especially now. I promise you, this plant will affect your life one day. We never know the future, and somehow it seems we do create it.

My observation has shown me we all learn through love or pain. If we choose fear, our lessons will be painful. If we choose love and wisdom, our lessons will be joyful. I hope you choose joy.

Either way, we are going to learn.

<u>Acknowledgements:</u>

Special thanks to Josh McCrimmon, Bridget Cook-Burch, Salenta Fox, Michael & Debra Bernoff, Morgan Steward, Hannah Lyon, Alexis Sparks, Ingrid Walton, Susan & Blain Jackson, Launa Moser. Without you this book would never have come to be.

Made in the USA
San Bernardino, CA
11 May 2020